DOCKSIDE

STAGE 1

BOOK 6

LET ME IN

John Townsend

RISING STARS

Liz Hill was in a bad mood.

Taz is late. Too late.

If he's not in soon, I'll go mad.
He hasn't got a key.

Psst.
Sky. Let me in.

New Message
From: Taz
Let me in.
Don't tell mum.
ntacts
GHI
MNO
4 GHI
9 WXYZ
8 TUV
7 PQRS

New Message
From: Sky
Mum is in a BAD MOOD.

New Message
From: Taz
LET ME IN but ssh.
ntacts
GHI
MNO
4 GHI
9 WXYZ
8 TUV
7 PQRS

New Message
From: Sky
I'll let you in for £10.

New Message
From: Taz
Cool. Do it.
I'm off to the loo.

Sky let Taz in.

I'll zoom to my room.

Hi mum. I've been in my room.
Any food?